Claudia Taylor
(Lady Bird) Johnson

Claudia Taylor (Lady Bird) Johnson

★★★★★★★★★★★★★★★★★★★★★★

1912–

BY MARGOT F. HORWITZ

CHILDREN'S PRESS®
A Division of Grolier Publishing
New York   London   Hong Kong   Sydney
Danbury, Connecticut

To the memory of my parents, Clarence and Anne Freedman,
who gave me a love of history

Consultants: JOHN TIFF
                      Historian
                      Lyndon B. Johnson National Historical Park
                      LINDA CORNWELL
                      Learning Resource Consultant
                      Indiana Department of Education

Project Editor: DOWNING PUBLISHING SERVICES
Page Layout: CAROLE DESNOES
Photo Researcher: JAN IZZO

Visit Children's Press on the Internet at:
http://publishing.grolier.com

Library of Congress Cataloging-in-Publication Data
Horwitz, Margot F.
    Claudia Taylor (Lady Bird) Johnson, 1912–   / by Margot F. Horwitz
       p.   cm. — (Encyclopedia of first ladies)
    Includes bibliographical references and index.
    Summary: Presents a biography of the wife of the thirty-sixth president of the United
States, a major source of support for her family and an energetic First Lady who was dedicated
to Operation Head Start and the beautification of the nation.
    ISBN 0-516-20595-1
    1. Johnson, Lady Bird. 1912–   —Juvenile literature. 2. Presidents' spouses—United
States—Biography—Juvenile literature. [1. Johnson, Lady Bird, 1912–   . 2. First ladies.
3. Women—Biography.] I. Title
E848.J6H67   1998
973.923'092—dc21   97–48242
[B]   CIP
                                                          AC

Table of Contents

Claudia Taylor
(Lady Bird) Johnson

Introduction

* * * * * * * * * * * * * * * * *

In the introduction to her book, *Wildflowers Across America*, published well after she had left the White House, Lady Bird Johnson speaks of the role of the wife of the president of the United States—and how she viewed that role:

"The Constitution of the United States does not mention the First Lady. She is elected by one man only. The statute books assign her no duties; and yet, when she gets the job, the podium is there if she cares to use it. I did."

She was speaking about her years in the White House, when she used her position to focus attention

* * * * * * * * * * * * * * * * *

Doing Good

★ ★

Eleanor Roosevelt set the tone for First Ladies to become actively involved in social issues. She campaigned and worked for humanitarian causes during husband Franklin D. Roosevelt's presidency (1933–1945). By her example, modern First Ladies continue to use their talents and position to support important causes. Jacqueline Kennedy was an active patron of the arts. Lady Bird nurtured growing things—children and plants—with her interest in Head Start and the environment. Pat Nixon selected volunteerism as her focus. Betty Ford, wife of President Gerald Ford, suffered from breast cancer and made it her mission to educate American women about the disease. President Carter's wife Rosalynn sponsored the cause of mental health. Nancy Reagan gave us the slogan "Just Say No" in her campaign against drug and alcohol abuse. Barbara Bush promoted literacy. Hillary Rodham Clinton took up the banner of affordable health care for all Americans early in her husband's first term. Her long-standing concern for children's issues culminated in an award-winning book called *It Takes a Village.*

on the American environment, rural and urban. Like few other presidents' wives, Lady Bird Johnson carved out a unique role for herself—based on a love of the land that warmed a lonely childhood and remained a source of pleasure when she was a young wife and mother.

After she entered the White House, Lady Bird Johnson "began to think that I might now have the means to repay something of the debt I owed nature." Beginning in Washington, D.C., the "nation's front yard," she created an atmosphere of natural beauty that spread across the nation—from crowded inner-city communities to wide-open roadsides and highways.

Even after her White House years,

Lady Bird Taylor loved the land around Karnack, Texas, where she grew up. This view near Karnack shows a lovely field of wildflowers.

Lady Bird Johnson continues her work with the environment, sponsoring the National Wildflower Research Center. While she no longer has the support of President Lyndon Baines Johnson, who died in 1973, Lady Bird continues their joint crusade to improve and beautify the American landscape.

★ ★ ★ ★ ★ ★ ★ ★ ★ ★ ★ ★ ★ ★ ★ ★

CHAPTER ONE

Growing Up with Nature

✫ ✫ ✫ ✫ ✫ ✫ ✫ ✫ ✫ ✫ ✫ ✫ ✫ ✫ ✫

Lady Bird Johnson was born Claudia Alta Taylor in the East Texas town of Karnack on December 22, 1912. Her lifelong love of the pine trees, bayous, and wildflowers of her hometown provided the inspiration for her lifelong labor of love—to preserve the natural beauty of the American landscape.

Claudia's parents were Thomas Taylor and Minnie Patillo. Thomas, who had grown up in a family of poor dirt farmers in Alabama, met Minnie when she fell from her horse in front of him. Picking her up, Thomas immediately fell in love and asked her father for her hand in marriage. Although Mr. Patillo laughed at the

✫ ✫ ✫ ✫ ✫ ✫ ✫ ✫ ✫ ✫ ✫ ✫ ✫ ✫ ✫

Portrait of America, 1912: Modern America Takes Shape

✯ ✯ ✯ ✯ ✯ ✯ ✯ ✯ ✯ ✯ ✯ ✯ ✯ ✯ ✯ ✯ ✯ ✯ ✯ ✯

In 1912, the year Claudia Alta Taylor was born, New Mexico and Arizona joined the Union. Now, all the land in the continental United States, from the Atlantic to the Pacific, was divided into states. America took its modern shape.

Like Claudia's family, more than half of the country's 92.5 million people still lived in rural areas. But America's future seemed to be in the cities. Huge corporations there provided jobs for thousands of workers. Factories needed laborers; offices hired record numbers of secretaries. Soon, more Americans would live and work in the cities than anywhere else. From the hustle and bustle emerged a new middle class of people. They lived comfortably and were neither wealthy nor poor. Many of them were angry at the social conditions they saw around them. Called Progressives, they worked for social justice and reform. African-Americans still suffered terribly. Their lives had grown worse since Reconstruction. Most lived in the rural South under dismal conditions. Violence against them increased. Laws segregated black people from white society and made it difficult for them to vote.

America's new middle class, meanwhile, had time to enjoy life. They took vacations in their Model T Fords and flocked to baseball games. (Boston beat New York in the 1912 World Series.) More than 10 million Americans attended the movies each week. In a small town called Hollywood, the brand-new movie industry produced hundreds of short comedies to satisfy them. Americans loved dancing, too, especially to fast music. Young women jiggled and swayed to the Turkey Trot and the Bunny Hop, ignoring the disapproval of their elders. Poetry, literature, and art flourished. Artists began to experiment with new styles. Painters used bold colors and abstract patterns to capture the energy of urban life.

In April, the sinking of the luxury liner *Titanic* shocked the world. On its first voyage, the most modern, largest, and fastest steamship ever built struck an iceberg and went down with 1,500 people. The ship was traveling too fast in dangerous waters. Many people wondered if the modern world was, too.

thought of his daughter marrying this poor young man, Thomas was determined to win the woman he loved. He moved to Texas, built a successful grocery store, and within a few years came back to Alabama to marry Minnie.

Now a wealthy landowner—and the owner of a general store that sold everything from cornmeal to coffins—Thomas built his wife a large and beautiful home in Karnack. The house was filled with books important to the college-educated Minnie (and later a

Lady Bird's father, Thomas Taylor, owned this general store in Karnack, Texas.

Thomas Taylor, a wealthy landowner, built this large, beautiful home in Karnack for his wife, Minnie. Claudia (Lady Bird) Taylor was born here on December 22, 1912.

strong influence on her daughter). The family was delighted when Claudia was born after two sons. As a baby, she received the nickname "Lady Bird," from a nurse who said that she was "as purty as a lady bird!" The name has stayed with her ever since.

Minnie had a passionate interest in the arts. She went to Chicago almost every year for the opera season, and often listened to classical records at home. Mrs. Taylor was also an advocate of women's voting rights and the integration of whites and blacks—very unusual at that time throughout the Deep South.

Unfortunately, Minnie Taylor's health was never strong, and in 1917 she died after a fall during her last pregnancy. With his sons away at boarding school, Thomas Taylor tried at first to be both father and mother to

Texas, U.S.A.

★ ★

When Claudia Alta Taylor was born in 1912, Texas was the largest state in the Union. (Alaska is bigger, but it didn't become a state until 1959.) Covering an astonishing 262,000 square miles (678,580 square kilometers), Texas spans 800 miles (1,287 km) from north to south and 770 miles (1,239 km) from east to west. So vast is the territory that it could swallow up five or six average-sized states. While it shares a huge size with Alaska, Texas also has something in common with Hawaii, since both were independent countries before they became American states. After it separated from Mexico in 1836, the Republic of Texas remained independent. In 1845, it agreed to become America's twenty-eighth state. Over the years, Texas grew famous for its cotton, cowboys, cattle, and crude—oil, that is. A huge oil strike in 1901 set off a flurry of "wildcatting," or drilling for oil in unproven locations, all around East Texas. Finally, in 1930, not far from Lady Bird's hometown, wildcatters struck the great East Texas Oil Field—among the largest in the world—that would ensure the state's oil-rich future.

16

A General Story

* *

Lady Bird's father was undoubtedly a very important man in Karnack. As owner of the general store, he would have provided just about everything one could need from cradle to coffin, hard candy to horse collars. In earlier times, the store owner was the person who got other people together to trade the goods each produced. As manufacturing boomed in the nineteenth century, this important citizen would travel to wholesale markets and stock up for the whole town, as well as buy and transport goods produced by his customers. The job became a great deal easier when traveling salesmen, called "drummers," came to the store to sell their lines of goods. Lucky was the woman who happened along just as the salesman pulled up in his wagon; she would have first chance at new fabrics and "notions," or sewing things. If she needed molasses or other ingredients, the store clerk would measure it out of a barrel into the jar that she had brought, and he might give crackers from the cracker barrel to her children. Self-service and individual packaging came later. Nearly as important was the general store's role as small-town gathering spot. Around the central stove, or on benches on the front porch, farmers and other townsfolk would gather to trade news and socialize year in and out.

little Lady Bird. But within a short time, Lady Bird was sent to Alabama to live with her mother's sister, Aunt Effie. A year later, Lady Bird and Effie came back to Texas.

Her unmarried aunt was very kind to Lady Bird, and continued the child's exposure to good books, art, and music. Lady Bird memorized poems, which she could recite many years later. While the child loved her aunt, whom she considered her second mother, Lady Bird was content to spend much of her time alone, roaming the countryside. She was never afraid because everyone knew her father, an important man, and they all looked out for the child.

Lady Bird enjoyed paddling on Caddo Lake, where she was surrounded by cypress trees hung with Spanish moss.

Old Port Caddo Road near Karnack

Blooming dogwood on the Taylor estate in Karnack

18

Lady Bird as a high schooler

Lady Bird attended Marshall High School in Marshall, Texas.

Lady Bird enjoyed each season, but was particularly happy when spring came to Karnack. She loved walking in the woods to find violets and dogwood blossoms, and played a game where she named the first daffodil "the princess." Although Lady Bird did not have many playmates, she was content to listen to the wind in the pine trees, and paddle on Caddo Lake's dark bayous, with old cypress trees and Spanish moss creating a special place for her.

Living in the country, Lady Bird attended a one-room schoolhouse, on top of a red clay hill. Later, she went to Marshall High School and graduated at the age of fifteen. Her grades were excellent, but she was so shy that she was afraid to be chosen to give one of two graduation speeches. She somehow arranged to be the third-highest student in her class, escaping the honor she feared.

At fifteen, Lady Bird was too young to go to college. She studied for an extra year at St. Mary's Episcopal School for Girls, a junior college in Dallas, before moving to Austin to attend the University of Texas. In col-

19

In this photograph taken in the 1920s, when Lady Bird attended the University of Texas in Austin, the main building of the university can be seen at the end of University Avenue.

lege, she began to make friends, and became part of a lively social scene. She also learned how to dress more fashionably—something Aunt Effie had been unable to teach her.

College brought Lady Bird new challenges. She was a leader in many student organizations, and served as publicity manager for the Sports Association, which coordinated women's athletics. She earned a bachelor of arts degree in 1933 and stayed an extra year to get a journalism degree along with a second-grade teacher's certificate and training in typing and shorthand. Her first career goal was journalism because she thought it would be fun to travel the world. (A preview of her life to come!)

For a time, Lady Bird Taylor was a

reporter for the *Daily Texan*—she believed that forcing herself to ask questions at press conferences would help overcome her lingering shyness, which would remain part of her personality for some years.

One after-college project Lady Bird took on was the remodeling of her father's home. One day in 1934, she went to Austin to consult with an architect about the renovation. While there, she stopped to visit an old friend who was working at the University of Texas. As she chatted with her friend, Gene Boehringer, a tall, gangly young man came into the office to say hello. Lyndon Baines Johnson, a secretary to local congressman Richard Kleberg, was immediately impressed by Lady Bird and invited her to breakfast the next day.

Lady Bird did not agree to the date, but the next morning, after seeing the architect, she walked by the hotel where Lyndon was having breakfast. When he saw her, he ran outside and insisted that she join him. He took her for a drive, and spent the day telling her all about his plans for the future, and about his financial prospects.

Lady Bird's father and her Aunt Effie are shown on the steps of the Taylor home in Karnack.

It was obvious that the young man was charmed by her quiet good looks, common sense, and dependability— and by her ambition and need to excel. Within twenty-four hours of their meeting, Lyndon Baines Johnson had found the woman he wanted to marry—and he proposed.

Lady Bird Taylor was completely astonished by his boldness, but she was also attracted to him. As she was to say later, "I knew I had met something remarkable— I just didn't know quite what!"

Soon after their first meeting, Lady Bird invited Lyndon home to meet her father and Aunt Effie. Thomas Taylor was impressed with Johnson and said to his daughter, "You've brought home lots of boys—this time you've brought home a man!"

Despite her father's enthusiasm, Lady Bird was in a state of confusion over the whirlwind courtship and was

This photograph of Lady Bird Taylor was taken shortly before her marriage to Lyndon Baines Johnson on November 17, 1934.

Rebekah Baines Johnson, Lyndon's mother

not yet ready to make a commitment to her eager suitor. She met Lyndon's parents. She also met the grandmother of the congressman he worked for, who

Lyndon and Lady Bird during their honeymoon in Mexico

warned her not to make a mistake by turning down his marriage proposal.

Finally, Lyndon Johnson decided he had waited long enough. He came to visit Lady Bird in Karnack one day and told her that he wanted an answer right away. He said that unless she accepted his proposal immediately, she didn't love him. He would go away and not ask her again. Realizing that she was in love, Lady Bird accepted. That decided, they drove to San Antonio where Johnson's friend was able to get an instant marriage license.

Lyndon Baines Johnson and Lady Bird Taylor were married on November 17, 1934, at St. Mark's Episcopal Church with three witnesses. Having forgotten to get a wedding band, Lyndon sent a friend across the street to Sears, Roebuck to bring back several rings. Lady Bird chose a ring that cost $2.50.

The couple took a short trip to Mexico for their honeymoon and then traveled to Washington together. At the age of twenty-two, Lady Bird Taylor Johnson began her political education, which was to continue for thirty-five years.

CHAPTER TWO

A Bride in Washington

★ ★ ★ ★ ★ ★ ★ ★ ★ ★ ★ ★ ★ ★ ★ ★

As the wife of the hardworking, ambitious secretary to Congressman Richard Kleberg, Lady Bird realized that politics was an all-consuming passion to her husband. Their small apartment was always open to Lyndon's political friends and allies, and she was constantly called upon to entertain them—on a very small budget.

Lady Bird worked hard to be hospitable, sometimes at a moment's notice. Her husband would call suddenly and announce that he was bringing several people—or more—home for dinner. Lady Bird was always gracious, even when she literally had to stretch the soup

★ ★ ★ ★ ★ ★ ★ ★ ★ ★ ★ ★ ★ ★ ★ ★

Congressman Richard Kleberg

Early in her marriage, Lady Bird began to write a "to do" list in a notebook, as her husband suggested. This would become a lifelong habit; she loved to be able to cross out items she'd completed. This sense of organization—and of looking out for constituents' interests—was an ideal preparation for the life of a congressman's wife. By 1937, Lady Bird was involved with her first political campaign.

Finding a sudden opening in his congressional district, Lyndon decided to seek the seat in a special election. Realizing how important this was to her husband, Lady Bird borrowed against her inheritance to help finance the campaign. During the next few months, when Lyndon was traveling the district making speeches, she stayed in the background, making sure he had a warm meal and clean clothes for the next phase of his campaign.

Women rarely campaigned openly with their husbands in those days. But even if this had been a typical practice, Lady Bird Johnson could never have been involved. She was still

or stew with water. Having been brought up in comfort, if not wealth, she had to adjust to pinching pennies. But she was somehow able to pay the bills and have enough left over to buy a U.S. savings bond every month.

In her role as wife of a congressional secretary, Lady Bird acted as an escort to the voters of their Texas district. She took them all through Washington, showing them not only the usual sights, but also museums, battlefields, and historic places miles from the city. If a constituent asked about a location of special interest, Lady Bird immediately arranged a visit.

An aerial view of Capitol Hill as it looked in the 1930s, when Lady Bird showed Lyndon's constituents the sights of Washington, D.C.

Among the historic sites of the capital that Lady Bird showed to her Texas visitors were the Lincoln Memorial (above) and the White House (below).

painfully shy, and anxious to stay in the background whenever possible. People who knew her in those days were amazed to see the transformation that was to occur over the years, as Lady Bird became a seasoned campaigner who won many votes for her husband and his political party.

After the 1937 election, Lady Bird became very involved in her husband's work. She memorized the names of all the counties and became acquainted with the politicians in Lyndon's Texas district. She served as his "sounding board" on his plans for the region, and worked on a steady stream of correspondence.

This life continued for the next five years. Lyndon won two more congressional elections, and then lost his race for the U.S. Senate in 1941. Shortly afterward, with the nation involved in World War II, Lady Bird Johnson's life changed dramatically. Her husband was sent off to the West Coast on government business as a naval officer, and she suddenly found herself in charge of his congressional office.

Realizing that his official aides

During World War II, Lady Bird helped persuade government agencies to bring electrification and irrigation to rural areas of Texas. Lady Bird (right front) met with this group at Buchanan Dam.

In 1941, before he left to serve in the war, Lyndon Johnson lost his bid for a seat in the U.S. Senate.

were young and inexperienced, Lady Bird took over many of their duties. She continued to deal with constituents as she had before, reading every Texas paper to learn about births and deaths. She also worked with governmental departments and agencies, to persuade them to consider the Texas district for such important projects as military bases and rural electrification.

Frightened at first of her new

World War II: Fast Facts

WHAT: The second great global conflict

WHEN: 1939–1945

WHO: The Axis Powers, including Germany, Italy, and Japan, opposed the Allies, including Britain, France, and the Soviet Union. The United States entered the war on the Allied side in 1941 after the bombing by Japan of Pearl Harbor in Hawaii.

WHERE: Fighting raged throughout the Pacific Ocean and in the Atlantic as well as from Scandinavia to North Africa, and deep into the Soviet Union.

WHY: Chancellor Adolf Hitler set out to make Germany the most powerful country in the world and began by invading his European neighbors. Japan, Italy, and Germany pledged support to one another in 1940. When the United States declared war on Japan after the attack on Pearl Harbor in 1941, Germany and Italy declared war on the United States.

OUTCOME: The war ended in stages. Germany surrendered in May 1945. Japan surrendered after the United States dropped two atomic bombs there in August. More than 400,000 American troops died in battle; about 17 million on both sides perished.

Lyndon Johnson as a naval officer

responsibilities, Lady Bird soon gained confidence as she realized she was performing a vital function as liaison between Congressman Johnson and the people of his district who needed a link with government. She found herself talking to high officials, including those in President Roosevelt's cabinet. Her name got her in to see them, but once there, she had to be able to present her case.

With Lyndon Johnson in the South Pacific war zone, and not reachable, Lady Bird learned that she could be effective by herself. She located missing service people and secured armed forces bases for their Texas region. She never raised her voice— just smiled and made clear what she wanted. Most important, she learned she could solve problems in her own way, as she continues to do.

When Lyndon returned, Lady Bird left his office but realized that she now had the ability to earn her own living. She and her husband recognized that politics was an uncertain way of life, and that they needed a more secure financial base. Lady Bird also wanted to use her journalism degree in a growing

Lieutenant Commander Lyndon Baines Johnson (second from right) shakes hands with General Ralph Royce in New Guinea during World War II.

Waiting for Wiring

☆ ☆

In the early 1930s, almost all city and town dwellers had electricity in their homes, but only 10 percent of the nation's farms had electrical power. Life on most farms meant no washing machine or dryer, or electric lights, or power to pump water. No matter how farmers pleaded with private power companies, they could not persuade them to string power lines into rural areas. Power companies argued that farmers would not be able to pay the high cost of electricity and that too little business made the expense of building power lines unprofitable. Faced with this dilemma, the determined farmers formed cooperatives to provide electricity for themselves. The government helped. President Franklin D. Roosevelt created the Rural Electrification Administration (REA) in May 1935, headed by brilliant engineer Morris Cooke. He disputed the private power companies' claims and worked out the exact cost of building lines and distributing electricity. The REA loaned farmers money to provide themselves with power. The cooperatives not only worked, they became profitable and paid back the loans while crisscrossing the nation with the power lines needed to bring farm life into a new electrified era.

industry. The solution: the purchase of a radio station in February 1943.

The Austin radio station, KTBC, was in bad condition—in many ways. Lady Bird moved to Austin for six months to reorganize and oversee the staff as well as to make changes in programming and pay off old bills. She literally had to clean up the place, scrubbing the building, top to bottom, on her hands and knees. Working 18-hour days, Lady Bird bought new equipment, gave the staff higher salaries, and finally moved the station into larger quarters as she increased the size of its audience and its share of local advertising.

Lady Bird Johnson's efforts led the station into profitability within six months. She persuaded the Federal Communications Commission, which had given her control of the station, to allow them to operate 24 hours a day, and also to increase the transmission to 1,000 watts—quite powerful for that time.

Within ten years, with the radio station worth $500,000, Lady Bird applied for and received a television license. The station—KTBC-TV—had a monopoly in the area for more than a decade. Mrs. Johnson also bought television stations in Waco and Corpus Christi, Texas. With television gaining in popularity and technical sophistication, the Johnsons made a profit. Lady Bird was in charge of the KTBC Corporation until her husband became president, when their holdings went into a trust. (After he left office, she resumed an active role in the corporation.)

Although Lady Bird was becoming a successful career woman, she longed for a home and a family. After many years of apartment living, the Johnsons bought their first house in Washington in 1942. It had a vegetable garden and lovely flowers. The garden was the first one Lady Bird created herself, and she chose flowers that gave the most color for the least work. Zinnias, marigolds, daffodils, and lilacs were her favorites from childhood, and she enjoyed having them around her now that she finally had her own home.

There was also an apple tree that blew down in a storm. Lady Bird called a nurseryman to prop it up and

Radio Days

★ ★

Before television, cable, or the Internet, there was radio. By the time Lady Bird bought her Austin radio station, American families were used to gathering around the large radio console stationed in their living rooms to hear a huge variety of programming. Out of the box came the comedy stylings of Jack Benny and George Burns, thrilling adventure programs starring Captain Midnight and the Lone Ranger, and the first daytime soap operas, as well as music and news. Young children hung on every word of storytellers and followed faithfully the adventures of Little Orphan Annie. For the first time, Americans received breaking news as it happened. Pioneer newsman Edward R. Murrow brought World War II into people's living rooms with his roundup of reporters speaking from all over Europe. President Roosevelt used radio to speak straight to the people in his "fireside chats." While radio kept Americans informed, it also allowed them to escape for a few minutes the gloom of economic depression and the chaos of world war.

keep it alive. He didn't think it could be saved, but it was—and was still blooming when the Johnsons moved out fifteen years later.

Perhaps because she had lost her own mother at a young age, family was particularly important to Lady Bird Johnson. But it was not until she had been married for ten years and had suffered several miscarriages that Lady Bird gave birth to their first daughter, Lynda Bird, in March 1944. Three years later, in July 1947, Luci Baines was born. The family was complete, ready to move into new and exciting areas of life.

★ ★ ★ ★ ★ ★ ★ ★ ★ ★ ★ ★ ★ ★ ★ ★

CHAPTER THREE

New Worlds to Conquer

* * * * * * * * * * * * * * * * * *

By 1948, Lyndon Baines Johnson was again looking toward a larger arena—the U.S. Senate—and this time he was determined to get there.

The primary campaign was long and difficult, and Lady Bird worked tirelessly and creatively to help her husband. One day, she and Lyndon's family tore apart a phone book. Each took a section, then dialed one number after another to try to persuade the voter in Lyndon's favor. Over the years, Lady Bird had overcome much of her shyness and made many speeches—by herself and with her husband, as he traveled throughout the state.

* * * * * * * * * * * * * * * * * *

The Woman's Vote

✶ ✶

When LBJ ran for the Senate in 1948, he knew he needed to persuade women to vote for him. This seems obvious to us today, but at that time, women had been allowed to vote for only twenty-eight years. The battle for "suffrage" (the right to vote) had been a long one, which began in earnest in 1848. That year, the first Women's Rights Convention met at Seneca Falls, New York. The delegates drew up a statement demanding for women "immediate admission to all the rights and privileges which belong to them as citizens of the United States." Conditions for women changed slowly, however, and it wasn't until 1920 that a constitutional amendment was passed to give American women the vote. Lady Bird's own mother strongly supported women's right to vote but died before the law could be passed. As a result, Mrs. Taylor, mother of a future First Lady, never cast a vote for president.

Surprisingly, for several years after women achieved suffrage, little attention was paid to female voters. But as women became more used to their role as voters, male politicians began to seek ways to win their support. After all, women made up about half of the voting population! This often became the job of political wives. In 1948, as Lyndon ran for the Senate, he depended heavily on Lady Bird's help. In the world of politics, women had moved from symbols of liberty and motherhood to voters and campaigners. Soon, more and more of them would become officeholders in their own right.

Lady Bird became an even more active participant as Lyndon realized the need for the woman's vote. His wife discovered that she was as capable at making speeches as she had been at handling mail and supervising campaign workers. She proved a hardy campaigner, cheerful despite difficulties that would have discouraged others.

Lyndon with young supporters in Texas during his 1948 senatorial campaign

Senator-elect Johnson in the Senate restaurant.

The night before the election, Lady Bird was riding to San Antonio to make a speech. When the car skidded and overturned twice into a roadside ditch, Lady Bird picked herself up, borrowed a fresh dress, gave the speech, and rode back to Austin to appear with Lyndon at a rally. Her husband did not find out about the incident until that night, when he noticed the bruises on her body.

Lyndon Baines Johnson won the election and embarked upon a twelve-year career in the U.S. Senate. He

Lyndon with his mother after winning his second Senate election in 1954

quickly became minority leader of the Senate, then majority leader, and pursued an even more active life. He drove himself and his staff members at a furious pace, working as many as fourteen hours a day. In July 1955, he suffered a serious heart attack and was immediately hospitalized.

Lady Bird Johnson had been helping Luci with her eighth birthday party when she got the call about her husband's illness. She rushed to the hospital and remained there, in a room next to his, for six weeks, doing

Luci Baines (left) and Lynda Bird Johnson (second from left) help Speaker of the House Sam Rayburn blow out his birthday candles at a 1951 party.

Who Leads the Leaders?

★ ★ ★ ★ ★ ★ ★ ★ ★ ★ ★ ★ ★ ★ ★ ★ ★ ★ ★ ★

Together, both houses of the U.S. Congress include more than 530 representatives and senators. So many people with so much business to complete require a good organization and strong leadership to get anything done. In the Senate, where two senators from each state do their part to study bills and pass them into law, Democrats and Republicans choose "floor leaders" for their parties. The party with the most senators elects a *majority leader,* and the one with fewer chooses a *minority leader.* They also select assistant leaders who are known as *whips.* These strategists work hard to keep their parties united on the issues and keep communication open among individuals and factions. The majority leader manages the entire Senate by scheduling bills for discussion and keeping business moving on a daily basis. Because of his firm grasp of senatorial rules and processes (and

his intimidating physical presence), Lyndon Johnson built a reputation as a strong, efficient, and effective floor leader. In his first year as majority leader, he pushed the Senate to pass more bills than in the prior two years combined.

everything she could to help him return to health.

As he improved, Lyndon continued his convalescence at the LBJ Ranch, a Johnson City, Texas, property they had purchased from Lyndon's aunt in 1951. Lady Bird entertained the congresspeople, reporters, and others who were constantly dropping by. It was a full-time job, making certain that Lyndon

The Johnsons are shown here at the hospital shortly after Lyndon's heart attack in July 1955.

Lady Bird and Lyndon on the way to the ranch, where Lyndon would continue his convalescence

did not become overtired, and that he kept to a proper diet. Lady Bird was totally caught up in her role as wife and caregiver, although this private life did not last long.

Soon the majority leader was back in the Senate, enjoying what he called "the best job in government." But in 1960, during the Democratic National Convention, presidential nominee John F. Kennedy asked him to become his running mate. Although Johnson never wanted to become vice president, he realized that his place on the ballot might help the Democratic party win.

He agreed to run as the vice presidential candidate, and campaigned

In the spring of 1958, Lady Bird (third from left) gave a luncheon for members of the American Society of Newspaper Editors at 30th Place, the Johnson's first house in Washington.

The large Johnson family gathered to celebrate Christmas 1955 at the LBJ Ranch in Johnson City, Texas.

Lady Bird, Lyndon, and Lyndon's mother Rebekah are shown here in 1956.

Lyndon greets his daughters on his return from a 1956 campaign trip.

Lyndon and Lady Bird accept a "yellow rose of Texas" from a young admirer during a 1960 campaign stop in Sioux Falls, South Dakota.

actively, as did Lady Bird. With Jacqueline Kennedy absent from the campaign trail because of her pregnancy, Lady Bird vowed to do everything she could to help the ticket.

Lady Bird Johnson traveled 35,000 miles (56,326 km) in two months, making speeches and greeting voters throughout the country. She was particularly effective in the "whistle-stop" type of campaign by train. She traveled mostly through the southern states. She was so popular in her campaign tours, especially in Texas, that Robert F. Kennedy later commented

During the Johnsons' 1960 whistle-stop campaign, they made a stop in Greenville, South Carolina.

Lady Bird, shown here between huge Kennedy and Johnson posters, appeared at an October 1960 press conference in New York City.

that she had helped to win the state for the Kennedy-Johnson ticket. Because the Kennedy-Nixon election was very close, Lady Bird was gratified to have played her special role in the victory.

After the new president and vice president took office in January 1961, Lady Bird found herself busier than ever. With Mrs. Kennedy still recovering from the premature birth of John F. Kennedy Jr., Lady Bird took over many of the First Lady's responsibilities. She became her official representative at charity functions and entertained foreign visitors. She even accepted Mrs. Kennedy's Emmy award for her special White House Tour television program.

Vice President and Mrs. Johnson also served as ambassadors abroad. Besides frequently traveling to far-

Lyndon Johnson taking the oath of office as vice president of the United States, January 20, 1961

The Johnsons arrive at an inaugural ball.

Lady Bird in her office with secretary Bess Abell

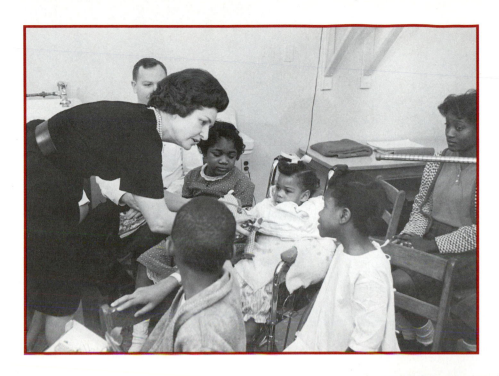

Lady Bird distributes Christmas toys to young patients at the Washington, D.C., General Hospital in December 1963.

flung regions of the world, Lady Bird and Lyndon Johnson often hosted foreign guests at The Elms, the vice-presidential home in Washington.

It was important to the vice president and his wife that visitors to the United States not think that all of America was like New York City—or even Washington, D.C. They were particularly delighted to host guests at the LBJ Ranch, which they had carefully restored.

Lady Bird's days as vice-presidential wife ended suddenly with the assassination of President Kennedy on

On a 1961 trip to the Philippines, Vice President and Mrs. Johnson are escorted to a state dinner.

The Johnsons were guests of Greek royalty in Corfu during a 1962 goodwill visit.

Lady Bird entertained Indira Gandhi, daughter of Indian Prime Minister Nehru, at The Elms.

Vice Presidents' Residence

✯ ✯

Everyone knows where the president lives, but what about the vice president? Not until 1974 did the "veep" and his family rate an official residence in Washington. Until then, they fended for themselves, living mostly in hotels or rented rooms. Several early "second men" hung their hats at the Willard Hotel. Established in 1850 just steps from the White House, the Willard was for years Washington's premier hotel. A more-recent version of it stands today. The Johnsons were lucky enough to afford their own house, called The Elms, a hilltop French-style chateau secluded by shrubbery. Finally, in 1974, Congress ordered that the admiral's house on the grounds of the U.S. Naval Observatory (an astronomical observation station) become the vice-presidential residence. Built in 1893 for the superintendent of the observatory, the thirty-three-room mansion underwent many needed repairs. In 1977, the Walter Mondales were the first second family to move into the official vice president's residence.

November 22, 1963, in Dallas, Texas. It was Mrs. Kennedy's first campaign trip with her husband as First Lady. The Johnsons had been traveling with the Kennedys in Texas. They had invited the Kennedys to the ranch for a few days of relaxation, including a festive barbecue, to culminate the four-day tour.

Riding behind the Kennedys during the fatal motorcade, the Johnsons raced to the hospital. As she stood in the hospital corridor trying to comfort Mrs. Kennedy, Lady Bird felt that she

During Christmas 1963, the Johnsons entertained the press at the LBJ Ranch.

Bashir Ahmad, a camel driver Lyndon met in Pakistan, was a guest at the ranch in the fall of 1961

West German Chancellor Konrad Adenauer (left) visited the LBJ Ranch in the spring of 1961.

A Sad Journey

★ ★

The hours following the assassination of President Kennedy must have been difficult indeed for Lady Bird and Lyndon. In that short time, and under the saddest and most shocking circumstances, they would be thrust into the role of first family of the United States. Moments after the president was declared dead, the Johnsons were whisked quietly to the Dallas airport, where *Air Force One*, the presidential jet, readied for departure. Curtains drawn, they waited on board for Mrs. Kennedy and the coffin to arrive. A local judge was summoned to administer to Lyndon the oath of office of president of the United States, as directed by the Constitution. There, as *Air Force One* waited on the runway to return to Washington, Lyndon Johnson, with Lady Bird and Jacqueline Kennedy at his side, was sworn in as chief executive. Mrs. Kennedy, who hadn't changed her clothes, was still wearing the pink suit stained with her husband's blood. In her diary, Lady Bird remembered Jackie's calmness and the silence of the return flight to Washington. By the time they arrived, the nation was reeling from news of the assassination. President Johnson stepped off the plane to lead a nation in deep mourning. "All that I have I would give gladly not to be here today," lamented Lyndon in his first speech to Congress as president.

Lyndon Johnson taking the oath of office aboard Air Force One

was "stalking across the stage in a Greek tragedy, just putting one foot in front of the other."

Meanwhile, Lady Bird's staff members had moved quickly into action. As the new president and his wife were returning to Washington from Dallas, Lady Bird's personal secretary Bess Abell rushed to The Elms from the ranch where she had been checking preparations for the Kennedy visit. Realizing that her secretary had not been to bed that night, Lady Bird exclaimed with her usual concern for others, "Oh, poor Bess—you've had no sleep at all!"

During the difficult holiday season that followed, Lady Bird substituted for Jacqueline Kennedy one last time, at the annual distribution of Christmas gifts to the Children's Wing of the Washington, D.C., General Hospital. Lady Bird realized she was stepping into a new phase of her life, with more responsibilities—and opportunities.

In 1941, Lady Bird had accompanied her husband to a reception in the Roosevelt White House for the

Bess Abell, Lady Bird's personal secretary, was an invaluable assistant to the new First Lady.

Duchess of Luxembourg. When they arrived home, she made a note in her diary that this might be their only visit to the White House. Years later, when she became a White House resident, not just a guest, she recorded her days and nights in a book that became *A White House Diary*. The moments happy and sad, major events and minor details, were all captured in this book, which no other First Lady had attempted.

★ ★ ★ ★ ★ ★ ★ ★ ★ ★ ★ ★ ★ ★ ★

CHAPTER FOUR

Life in the White House

⭐ ⭐ ⭐ ⭐ ⭐ ⭐ ⭐ ⭐ ⭐ ⭐ ⭐ ⭐ ⭐ ⭐ ⭐ ⭐

When Lady Bird Johnson abruptly found herself First Lady of the nation, she was overwhelmed. As she wrote in *A White House Diary*, "I feel like I am suddenly onstage for a part I never rehearsed."

Unlike most presidential wives, who have a transition from Election Day to the Inauguration, Lady Bird was immediately engulfed in a new life. Her days as a private person were over—she must now be an even stronger support and comfort to her husband as he grappled with his sudden new responsibilities.

She also had to keep the household on an even keel for Lynda and Luci, now in the midst of typically teen-

⭐ ⭐ ⭐ ⭐ ⭐ ⭐ ⭐ ⭐ ⭐ ⭐ ⭐ ⭐ ⭐ ⭐ ⭐ ⭐

When the Beatles Were Young

✶ ✶

Even though Luci did math homework in the White House Treaty Room and Lynda dated movie star George Hamilton, the first daughters lived fairly typical teenage lives. Theirs was an innocent "Pepsi Generation," according to the cola ads of the day; hippies, acid rock, and the counterculture were still a few years away. When her father took office in 1963, quiet Lynda was already a mature nineteen, but sixteen-year-old Luci bubbled over. After a new British rock group called the Beatles appeared on *The Ed Sullivan Show* in 1964, Luci explained sorrowfully to the press that her father wouldn't allow her to meet the "Fab Four" when they arrived at the Washington train station. In other music news, a youthful Bob Dylan made folk rock concerts—"hootenannies"—popular; girl groups such as the Supremes belted out the beat of Motown; and California launched the surf songs of the Beach Boys. "Watusi" Luci loved to dance; the watusi, the twist, the frug, and the mashed potato came and went. It was difficult for the girls to socialize, however. Pestered by the press and shadowed by Secret Service agents, Lynda and Luci often brought their dates home to the White House for peace and quiet. "It takes guts to date them," observed one brave suitor.

aged lives. Early on, Lady Bird recognized that she would have many pulls on her energies. In one diary entry, she wrote, "If I'm going to win the battle to keep us all close together, I'll need to apply equal time to the girls, along with Lyndon's business, and my public duties, and my own pursuits."

The five and one-half years in the White House were a test of that determination, but by the time the Johnsons went back to Texas, she could look back with satisfaction on their lives together—and on the development of her daughters' personal lives.

An important move toward keeping the family close was Lynda's deci-

The four Johnsons at the LBJ Ranch on Christmas Day, 1963

Lynda Bird Johnson (right) and a friend on the first day of classes at George Washington University

sion to transfer from the University of Texas to George Washington University, so that she could live in the White House and be available when her parents needed her. At age sixteen, Luci remained at the National Cathedral School in Washington.

Lady Bird realized that life in Washington could be a strain on youngsters, at any age. She recalled Lynda as a young child complaining "Mama, Washington is sure meant for the congressmen and their wives—but it is not meant for their children." When the girls became young women, though, they found their lives in the White House interesting and fun, despite occasional problems.

During their father's years as president, the young women often acted as

Lynda Bird (right) chats with Princess Benedikte of Denmark at a 1965 White House tea.

Lynda Bird, acting in place of her mother, presented the Margo Jones Award to these individuals for carrying on the tradition of encouraging new plays and new playwrights.

hostesses for a variety of official functions, and took visitors on tours. It was exciting for them to meet the heads of state of many nations, as well as former presidents and other dignitaries. But they were also able to entertain their own friends in the big house, and Lady Bird was always pleased to see the White House—their home— filled with young people.

The friendly and outgoing Johnson daughters enjoyed an active social life—as well as the constant attention of the press. Luci seemed not to mind these attentions to her social life, but

Luci Baines entertains underprivileged children at a 1965 White House Christmas party.

Lynda Bird with the "healthiest boy and girl in Japan"

Luci at a party for children of the diplomatic corps

Lynda at a White House lawn carnival for children

Lady Bird greets garment workers in Wilkes-Barre, Pennsylvania, a town in a coal-mining area that was wracked by poverty and unemployment in 1964.

Lynda was often annoyed by what she considered an embarrassing invasion of her privacy.

Lady Bird herself soon developed a close relationship with the White House press corps. With her background in journalism and politics, Lady Bird was sensitive to the needs of the media people, and worked well with them. She became particularly close to the "ladies of the press," and enjoyed many trips with them during her stint as First Lady.

One of Lady Bird Johnson's first and most significant official trips was to Wilkes-Barre, Pennsylvania. It was

Lady Bird touring a fabric mill during her trip to Wilkes-Barre

Poverty speech. And flying over the once-lovely countryside now stripped by mining, Lady Bird observed that "God had done His best by this country, but Man has certainly done his worst, and now it is up to Man to repair the damage."

This journey was the first of many well-organized, well-publicized trips on which Lady Bird set a fast pace. With a style reminiscent of Eleanor Roosevelt, the First Lady with whom she is often compared, she developed a personality of her own, giving 164 speeches and making 70 appearances during her years in the White House.

Soon after he took office, President Johnson faced the decision of whether or not to run for his own term. He had many doubts, which he voiced to his wife. They discussed the situation thoroughly, but she put her beliefs on paper right before the Democratic Convention:

"You are as brave a man as Harry Truman, or FDR, or Lincoln. You have been strong, patient, determined beyond any words of mine to express. I honor you for it . . . to step out now would be wrong for the country . . . I

in this coal-mining region that she took notice of problems that were to play a major role during her White House years: poverty and the scarring of the landscape. The depressed economy and unemployment in the region were typical of the ills the president had just addressed in his War on

Another Globe-Trotting First Lady

★ ★ ★ ★ ★ ★ ★ ★ ★ ★ ★ ★ ★ ★ ★ ★ ★ ★ ★ ★

Upon moving into the White House, Eleanor Roosevelt told a reporter, "There isn't going to be any First Lady. There is just going to be plain, ordinary Mrs. Roosevelt." Eleanor turned out to be neither. She traveled and campaigned tirelessly for human rights, equality for women and blacks, and humanitarian causes. While Franklin Roosevelt was president in the 1930s and 1940s, Eleanor covered thousands of miles a year, visiting the coal mines of Pennsylvania and the cornfields of the Midwest. During World War II, she took a five-week trip to visit wounded soldiers in the South Pacific. After Franklin Roosevelt's death, President Truman appointed Eleanor to the United Nations, where she worked very hard for war refugees. In 1952, she accepted an invitation from India's prime minister and vis-

ited not only that country but managed to "drop in" on the leaders of Lebanon, Syria, Jordan, and Pakistan. She visited Japan, meeting Emperor Hirohito and his wife, the Empress Nagako. She saw firsthand the devastation at Hiroshima, where Americans had dropped the atom bomb in 1945. In 1957, she traveled throughout the Soviet Union, ending her trip with a visit to Premier Nikita Khrushchev whom she interviewed for the *New York Post*. Such boundless energy inspired Lady Bird Johnson, who knew and greatly admired the remarkable Mrs. Roosevelt.

First Lady Eleanor Roosevelt boarding an airplane

can't carry any of the burdens . . . so I know it's only *your* choice."

Lyndon Johnson was always eager to hear his wife's views. As he once commented: "Through our years together, I have come to value Lady Bird's opinion of me, my virtues, and flaws. I have found her judgment generally sound."

Lady Bird firmly believed that leaving the presidency then would have been wrong for the nation and would have shown its citizens that Lyndon did not have courage. When he agreed to run, Lady Bird threw herself into the campaign. She traveled throughout many parts of the country, especially the South.

Riding a train—the Lady Bird Special—she made a whistle-stop tour covering 1,682 miles (2,707 km), with forty-seven stops and four "slowdowns." The southern states were a concern because of the president's liberal views on civil rights, but Lady Bird made the people there feel that Lyndon was one of them. As in 1960, Lady Bird made a real difference.

Whether campaigning around the country or planning White House

Members of the press surround the Johnsons as they walk their dogs on the White House lawn.

The First Lady covered many miles on her whistle-stop campaign tour aboard the Lady Bird Special.

Lady Bird giving one of her many speeches during the 1964 presidential campaign

events large and small, Lady Bird Johnson was an energetic First Lady who threw herself completely into her responsibilities. She often said that she felt totally supported by her husband in all of her activities.

Lyndon and Lady Bird Johnson were a team. He had urged her to use her power as First Lady to get things done, and not "fritter away her time." He suggested that she pick a few projects and make them happen. Choosing two vital issues that were to make a lasting impact on the nation—Head Start and beautification—Mrs. Johnson came to realize that she had a forum from which she could make a difference. Her efforts went even further than she expected; her issues were to make an impact that continues thirty years later.

Lady Bird and Lyndon at the President's boyhood home in Johnson City

☆ ☆ ☆ ☆ ☆ ☆ ☆ ☆ ☆ ☆ ☆ ☆ ☆ ☆ ☆ ☆

CHAPTER FIVE

Offering a Head Start in Life

* * * * * * * * * * * * * * * *

After the election of 1964, which Lyndon Baines Johnson won in a landslide against Senator Barry Goldwater, Lady Bird began to move into her own distinct areas of activity.

One of her first projects was the government program Operation Head Start. In this, she worked with Sargent Shriver of the Office of Economic Opportunity. Head Start was concerned with 100,000 underprivileged children ages five and six. It gave them a medical examination, a free meal, and pre-school education, and followed through to preserve their gains in their first years of school.

* * * * * * * * * * * * * * * *

Barry Goldwater (1909–1998)

★ ★

Although they were political opposites, Texan Lady Bird Johnson and Arizonan Barry Goldwater had some things in common. Both grew up in the West, members of pioneer families who made their wealth running stores. Both celebrated the natural beauty of their home states. Like Lady Bird, Barry was a savvy businessperson before he turned his interests to politics. He rose in his family's department-store business from clerk to chairman of the board. He took measures to better the jobs of the people working for him, instituting health insurance and profit sharing. In 1952, he was elected to the U.S. Senate, where he served on and

off until his retirement in 1987. His love of Arizona's landscape and native cultures was always a great influence in Goldwater's life. His photographs of Arizona's scenes and people were published in *The Face of Arizona* and *People and Places*. In matters of politics, however, Senator Barry Goldwater could not have disagreed more with the Johnsons. A leader among the most conservative Republicans, Goldwater always believed the federal government should stay out of people's lives almost completely.

Lady Bird (second from left behind flag) and Sargent Shriver (right) at a Head Start ceremony

Also included were dental care, inoculations, and hearing and speech tests. While the eight-week course for each child was short, Lady Bird was firm about "having to start somewhere to break the cycle." Along with teachers, many volunteers—often parents of the children—were trained to work as aides in the classroom.

Head Start became a top priority for President Johnson. As a former educator, he had seen how children could be influenced in their earliest development. In his book *Vantage Point*, Lyndon Johnson noted that "most of a child's full potential is achieved before school age. Half of the child's eventual capacity is established by the age of four. By six, two-thirds of the adult intelligence has been formed."

The Johnsons were also enthusias-

Sargent Shriver (1915–)

★ ★

R. Sargent Shriver married Eunice Mary Kennedy, future president John Kennedy's sister, on May 23, 1953. However, it was Joseph Kennedy, John and Eunice's father, who first noticed the young journalist. Joseph gave him a job managing a new Kennedy business investment in Chicago, the Chicago Merchandise Mart, which was the largest commercial building in the world at that time. Rising in Chicago to head the Board of Education, Shriver halted his own career to aid John Kennedy's first presidential campaign. This sacrifice served him well when Kennedy won the presidency and asked Shriver to administer what would become one of JFK's greatest creations: the Peace Corps. Advertised as "the toughest job you'll ever love," the Peace Corps sends skilled young Americans to third-world countries, the least economically advanced. There, they are teamed with inhabitants of the countries to fight disease and improve public health facilities, work on agricultural and construction projects, and teach language and business skills. Sargent Shriver's daughter, news correspondent Maria, is married to muscular Austrian actor Arnold Schwarzenegger. The couple has four children.

tic about Head Start because it reached a culturally deprived population lacking in everything from toys and books to crayons, paints, and paper. Studies showed that many of the children, especially those from inner cities, couldn't even recognize pictures of animals from a zoo. The only animal they could recognize immediately was a rat.

There was no question in the First Lady's mind that real strides could be made in this area. It was an aspect of the war on poverty that people could really understand. Lady Bird was particularly hopeful that young children whose families rarely talked to them at home could be taught to communicate through simple teaching of vocabulary and manners.

Lady Bird took an active interest in Head Start, visiting schools and day-care centers around the country to oversee the program's growth. In New Jersey, the first state to enlist in Head Start, she was excited to see two examples of the program at work: one in a congested Newark slum and another in a poor rural area. In both cases, the children's narrow worlds opened up quickly, as they learned how to pay attention to the teacher, get along with other youngsters, and speak in language that "went beyond grunts and profanity."

A mother, a volunteer in a New Jersey program, described one student

Lady Bird greets children in New Jersey, the first state to enlist in the Head Start program.

Pancho's Story

★ ★

One clear example of the value of the Head Start program is the story of Pancho, a young Mexican-American boy who had been helped by a Head Start project in California. Pancho had been listless and uninterested in learning as the result of a serious thyroid condition. This condition was discovered by a member of the Head Start medical team in his community and was quickly corrected. The boy's progress became the subject of a film, which was shown often around the nation. The film was first screened at the White House, and Pancho, the guest of honor, was a lively youngster who showed no trace of his former medical problem.

Lady Bird (waving), Governor Richard J. Hughes (holding hands with children), and Sargent Shriver (hatless, behind Lady Bird) on their way to Cleveland Elementary School in Newark, New Jersey

who had come in silent and listless, uninterested in her surroundings. Within five or six weeks she had become a happier, involved child. One day, she reached up to take the woman's hand and said, possibly for the first time in her life, "I love you."

During its twenty-fifth-year celebration in 1990, statistics proved that more than 11 million low-income preschoolers and their families had benefited from Head Start's extensive child development program. There is documented evidence of the program's success, both in educational achievement and in creating the social competence children need at home, in school, and in their communities.

Head Start's success goes beyond children's needs by also helping their families. The program offers career training and employment, resulting in new jobs in 2,000 communities across the nation. It also plays a major role in providing and coordinating local social and health services for disadvantaged families.

A difference is also obvious within the individual family structure. Because of the emphasis on parental involvement, Head Start parents realize that they are not only their chil-

Lady Bird (third from right) joins a Head Start panel discussion at Cleveland Elementary School in Newark.

dren's most important teachers, but also their decision-makers. A sense of parental responsibility is created, as well as a feeling of trust within members of the family.

Over the years, Head Start has supported many demonstration projects to encourage communities to create new ways of addressing the needs of low-income families with young children and to enhance their quality of life. It is interesting to see that the program has changed with the times to become even more responsive to the needs of families as they work to become self-sufficient.

During the twenty-fifth anniversary celebration, the Commissioner of the Administration for Children, Youth and Families condensed the meaning of Head Start into a few meaningful words, noting that nearly 500,000 children each year find a few hours when they can enjoy being kids: "A childhood for every child: this is our motto."

CHAPTER SIX

Beauty in the Environment

During her childhood in Texas, Lady Bird Johnson had developed a deep love of the land and the environment. When her husband spoke of a Great Society in which Americans would clean up the air and water and preserve the shrinking wilderness and green spaces in their cities, she decided to put her personal feelings to work.

As Lady Bird noted in the introduction to her book on wildflowers, "Because my heart had for so long been in the environment, I began to think that in the White House I might now have the means to repay something of the debt I owed nature for the enrich-

The Great Society

★ ★

President Johnson had a vision of a "Great Society that rests on abundance and liberty for all." Though on the surface, America seemed a comfortable and wealthy nation, research in the early 1960s revealed that one-fifth of the population lived in poverty. Suffering most were African-American families, the elderly, and households headed by women. Under the banner of the Great Society, Johnson declared an all-out "War on Poverty." Between 1964 and 1966, he pushed through scores of bills to improve the living conditions of poor Americans. The Great Society created hundreds of landmark programs. New laws banned discrimination and extended voting rights. Medicare and Medicaid provided health care for the elderly and the poor. The Job Corps trained the underprivileged in work skills. Head Start gave impoverished preschoolers a jump on their educations. The Department of Housing and Urban Development oversaw housing for the poor. Its secretary, Robert Weaver, was the first African-American in the president's cabinet. Schools received major federal funding for the first time. The first laws were passed to clean up the environment. And on and on. There were so many reforms that the government couldn't afford them all. To this day, the funding—and value—of the Great Society remains controversial. One thing is certain, however. During the 1960s, the "War on Poverty" brought hope to millions, reducing the percentage of poor Americans in the population by nearly half.

ment provided from my childhood onward."

In February 1965, Lady Bird and Secretary of the Interior Stewart Udall brought together a group of interested people—philanthropists, designers, publishers, government officials, and civic leaders—to form the Committee for a More Beautiful Capital.

One of the committee's early projects was planting flowers throughout

Lady Bird, standing at the Treasury Building, discusses the beautification of the capital.

Washington, D.C., and encouraging businesses to landscape their own areas. The plan was two-fold: to beautify the tourist areas around the monuments and to bring beauty to the inner city.

The Committee for a More Beautiful Capital organized clean-up and fix-up projects, and worked to improve school yards and playgrounds. Because Mrs. Johnson and her colleagues realized the need for community participation, they set up annual awards for people who did outstanding work in neighborhoods, businesses, and public spaces. Hundreds of children were among the many people honored for their efforts.

Many of the projects were small in scale, but the First Lady believed that ordinary citizens could do much to improve the world around them—by reducing litter, planting trees and flowers, and caring for their surroundings. She believed that beautification and revitalization could unite a city, bringing economic growth, old-fashioned neighborliness, and a sense of pride.

Lady Bird recalled the day she

One of the projects of the Committee for a More Beautiful Capital was repairing and landscaping public schools in the city. Lady Bird is shown here planting tulips at a Washington, D.C., school.

noticed a ravine in a suburb of Washington filled with rotting tires, old refrigerators, and "all the debris of a careless civilization." She remarked happily that within a year, everything changed. Citizens raised money to haul away forty truckloads of junk, to landscape, and to plant. It became an outdoor living area that the entire community could enjoy.

In another location, thirty-seven blocks were organized: merchants were persuaded to contribute paint,

brushes, rakes, shovels, and brooms. One summer week, 1,000 boys and girls and 200 adults helped clean out the trash and create an entirely new look for the low-income community.

The Committee for a More Beautiful Capital was concerned about the look of local public schools with broken windows and peeling paint. Local nurseries, foundations, and generous donors helped science and art teachers and schoolchildren to revitalize their learning environment. The students

Lady Bird planting an ornamental pear tree in Washington

responded with pride, rather than vandalism. As their physical environment improved, so did their self-esteem.

One young resident of Washington, D.C., symbolized the excitement of the new approach to community beautification. In April 1965, John Hatcher wrote to the White House requesting an azalea plant to help his yard look better. Azalea plants were sent to the young man,

and to many city neighborhoods. Bleak, bare areas soon turned into blooming, vibrant communities.

The committee made significant contributions to Washingon, mostly by improving what was already there. The group landscaped hundreds of park sites, schools, and playgrounds, and planted nearly 2 million bulbs, 83,000 spring-flowering plants, 50,000 shrubs, 25,000 trees, and 137,000 annuals.

Lady Bird Johnson believed that beautification meant "total concern for the physical and human quality we pass on to our children and the future." It includes clean water, clean air, clean roadsides, safe waste disposal, and preservation of valued old landmarks—as well as great parks and wilderness areas. President Johnson worked hard to pass early legislation on water and air pollution, on clean rivers, on highway beautification, and on the preservation of wilderness areas.

Although she worked behind the scenes, preferring to let her husband use political means to get it done, Lady Bird Johnson was so instrumen-

Secretary of the Interior Stewart Udall (left) and Lady Bird (right) hiked in Big Bend National Park during a trip designed to focus attention on the need to preserve valuable parks and wilderness areas.

tal in passing the Highway Beautification Act of 1965 that many people in Congress called it the "Lady Bird Act." Impetus for the act grew out of Lady Bird's distress at the abandoned cars and ugly billboards she saw during her many trips between Texas and Washington.

Congress stood up to strong opposition from the billboard lobby. In addition to limiting billboards on federal highways, the act encouraged better planning of the nation's roads to improve the landscape for people traveling by car throughout the country. Walter Reuther of the AFL-CIO labor union spoke for many in wishing that his workers, who could not afford to fly to elegant areas, would have pleasant surroundings closer to home.

Lady Bird's energy seemed endless in her drive to improve the look of the nation, starting with Washington, D.C. She also dedicated new parks and gardens in ceremonial tree and flower plantings throughout the nation and gave speeches emphasizing the connection between ugliness and crime.

Visiting beautification projects throughout the nation, Lady Bird Johnson gave presidential recognition to citizens working to improve their communities. She traveled 200,000 miles (321,860 km) for these causes, calling attention to campaigns to improve the American landscape. The First Lady was many years ahead of her time in working for public-private partnerships of government, citizens, and academic institutions that would plan and work together.

An involved business community brought a new perspective and action. The Giant Food Company opened a store in a Washington inner-city area and planted trees and flowers in a vest-pocket park on the property. The manager and all the employees were from the neighborhood.

The company received a beautification award in 1967. One year later, during major rioting following the death of Martin Luther King Jr., none of the Giant food stores was harmed. The company's work with the African-American community and its

Lady Bird (second from right) rafting with Stewart Udall (right) on the Rio Grande in Big Bend National Park

Lady Bird meets with the Ridgecrest Community Project volunteers in St. Petersburg, Florida.

The First Lady (right) admires the flowering plants at the Plaza Hotel in New York City.

beautification efforts had shown its good faith with the neighborhood.

Throughout her tenure as First Lady, Lady Bird Johnson made an effort to put beautification into a larger setting. She emphasized quality-of-life issues, the larger problems that "beautification" did not always describe. In many ways, her work anticipated the ecological efforts that began in the 1970s. Lady Bird's passionate interest in the world around her did not stop after the White House years.

During the 1967 National Governors Association meeting in Washington, D.C., the First Lady (second from left) hosted the governors' wives on a beautification bus tour of the capital.

Acting in Anger

★ ★

The assassination of Martin Luther King Jr., on April 4, 1968, shocked the nation. While most Americans, black and white, mourned peacefully and quietly for the great civil-rights leader and apostle of nonviolence, others acted out their rage on the streets. In 168 cities and towns, mobs looted and set stores on fire. In the capital, 10 people were killed and more than 700 fires raged. National Guard troops were deployed to protect the White House and the Capitol. The rioting lasted for three days and nights. In all, 46 people were killed and $45 million worth of damage was done to property throughout the nation.

CHAPTER SEVEN

Home to Texas

★ ★ ★ ★ ★ ★ ★ ★ ★ ★ ★ ★ ★ ★ ★ ★ ★ ★

The Johnsons had moved into another phase of life when both daughters married and gave birth to their first children while Lyndon Johnson was president. In August 1966, Luci married Patrick Nugent and a reception was held at the White House. Their son, Patrick Lyndon (Lyn) was born in June 1967. In a White House military wedding in December of that year, Lynda married Captain Charles Robb. She gave birth to a daughter, Lucinda, in October 1968.

The joy of becoming grandparents was tempered for Lyndon and Lady Bird Johnson by the departure of both young fathers for service in the Vietnam War.

★ ★ ★ ★ ★ ★ ★ ★ ★ ★ ★ ★ ★ ★ ★ ★ ★ ★

Vietnam War: Fast Facts

WHAT: Conflict over control of the Southeast Asian nation of Vietnam

WHEN: 1957–1975

WHO: The United States, South Vietnam, and various allies opposed the North Vietnamese and the Viet Cong

WHERE: Throughout North and South Vietnam, and later into Cambodia and Laos

WHY: In the early 1950s, the French controlled Vietnam. Fearing a Communist takeover of Vietnam and the rest of Southeast Asia, American leaders supported the French. When the French withdrew, the United States sent military advisers to help train the South Vietnamese to oppose the Communist north. America became more and more involved until U.S. troops were actually fighting alongside the South Vietnamese in a war against North Vietnam.

OUTCOME: Direct American military involvement ended with a cease-fire in 1973. In all, 58,000 American soldiers and about 1 million North and South Vietnamese perished. In 1975, the North invaded the South, and the capital of Saigon surrendered. Today, a unified Vietnam lives under Communist rule.

The realization that the Nugent and Robb families were like thousands of others separated by military duty was a personal aspect of the Vietnam War burden with which the president struggled for many years. It was his hope for an end to the war that prompted Johnson not to run for reelection in 1968.

In January 1969, Lyndon and Lady Bird Johnson left the White House and returned to their native Texas.

For the champion of beautification, coming home was a shocking experience. She noticed that houses and highways had taken the place of the fields, pastures, and wild lands she had loved for their openness. She went right to work, helping Austin's citizens build a hiking trail along the town "lake"—part of the Colorado River that runs through the city's downtown area. Before the task was finished, the team had turned an overgrown eyesore and deserted dump area into a wide path dotted with wildflowers.

Late in 1969, Lady Bird also sponsored the first of an annual series of beautification awards to members of the Texas Highway Department in cer-

Luci Baines Johnson, shown here with her parents, married Patrick Nugent in 1966.

In 1967, Lynda Bird Johnson married Charles Robb in a White House military wedding.

Lyndon Baines Johnson's boyhood home is now part of the Lyndon B. Johnson National Historical Park.

Lady Bird and Lyndon at the dedication of the LBJ State Park in Stonewall, Texas

emonies at LBJ State Park. The awards recognized the use of wildflowers and roadside parks and maintenance of roadside plants and shrubs, direct results of the 1965 Highways Act. Mrs. Johnson wanted the awards to "help make preservation and propagation of national assets an ongoing aim."

Lady Bird spent most of the next few years with her husband, who had time to relax and reflect on his life in politics—a life he described in his book *Vantage Point*. Lyndon Johnson made few political appearances, so was able to enjoy his home and his growing family. Lynda and Luci presented their parents with a total of seven grandchildren. But the former president did not live long after leaving office. In January 1973, he died of heart disease at the age of sixty-five.

For a period after her husband's

Lyndon with his first grandchild, eleven-month-old Patrick (Lyn) Nugent

death, Lady Bird lived very quietly. Her health was not good, and she seemed depressed by the loss of her life's companion. Gradually, however, she began to take on new responsibilities. She raised funds for a series of symposiums on education, the arts, civil rights, women in public life, and environmental issues. They were held at the LBJ Library and Museum in Austin.

Lady Bird also continued her membership on the Board of Regents of her alma mater, the University of Texas. She took board positions with the National Geographic Society, the National Park Service, and the American Conservation Association.

Lady Bird did not leave politics behind completely. In 1976, she cam-

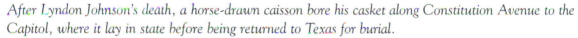

After Lyndon Johnson's death, a horse-drawn caisson bore his casket along Constitution Avenue to the Capitol, where it lay in state before being returned to Texas for burial.

Lady Bird campaigned for son-in-law Charles Robb when he ran for lieutenant governor of Virginia.

paigned for democratic candidates, especially her son-in-law Charles S. Robb as he sought and won the office of lieutenant governor of Virginia. He was later to become governor, and then a U.S. senator from that state. Mrs. Johnson also participated in the "Salute to America" program, reading excerpts from the Declaration of Inde-

pendence to audiences in the United States and Canada.

The former career woman also resumed an active role in the corporation owning the KTBC radio and television stations, and increased her duties after the death of her business manager in 1977.

Fifteen years after leaving the White House, Lady Bird Johnson was still involved with the cause of national beauty. She had an ongoing concern with making Americans conscious of the appearance of roadsides, and spoke out often for standards of regulation to enhance national beauty.

In the early 1980s, the LBJ Library and Museum in Austin was the setting for a conference on national beauty and the nation's unfinished environmental agenda. Participants included many of the activists from the 1960s, who believed that the original conference had been a bridge from traditional ideas on conservation to the modern environmental movement.

Perhaps the most important national beauty project undertaken by Lady Bird Johnson in her years after the White House has been the founding of the National Wildflower Research Center in 1982. It was an idea that had taken root during the Texas Highway Department ceremonies honoring those who planted and maintained wildflowers and roadside plants, but it went way beyond its home region to encourage the growth and cultivation of wild plants and flowers throughout the United States.

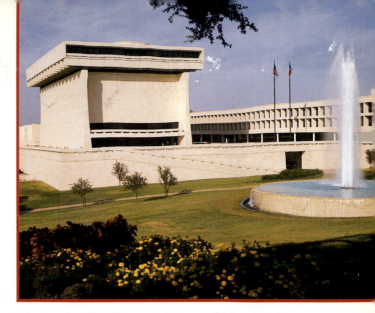

The Lyndon B. Johnson Library and Museum in Austin, Texas

The World for Everyone

✸ ✸

On January 13, 1888, thirty-three men gathered in Washington, D.C., with a single purpose. They hoped to create an institution that would both explore the world's geography and share its wonder with ordinary people everywhere. All were experienced men in many ways, but they were not all geographers or even scientists. The National Geographic Society, with more than 9 million members, is now the largest scientific and educational society in the world. The society has supported such news-making projects as the polar expeditions of Robert E. Peary and Richard E. Byrd, archaeologist Howard Carter's discovery of King Tutankhamen's tomb in Egypt, and the work of French undersea explorer Jacques Cousteau. Through *National Geographic*, the first magazine to focus on spreading scientific knowledge through photography and easy-to-read text, and more recently through television and classroom productions, the society brings the thrill of scientific exploration and discovery to life for the average person.

CHAPTER EIGHT

Planting Wildflowers Everywhere

* * * * * * * * * * * * * * * *

Lady Bird Johnson founded the National Wildflower Research Center (NWRC) on her seventieth birthday—December 22, 1982.

The former First Lady gave her reasons to a reporter. Noting that her children, grandchildren, and family business were "all on an even keel . . . all my years of trying to help Lyndon are over. The LBJ Library is well established. The LBJ School of Public Policy at the University of Texas is doing all right. The River Park beautification project in Austin is doing well. There aren't that many active years left. If I were ever to do anything on my own, I should do it now."

* * * * * * * * * * * * * * * *

A field of wild poppies at the National Wildflower Research Center outside Austin, Texas

The National Wildflower Research Center was founded by Lady Bird Johnson in 1982.

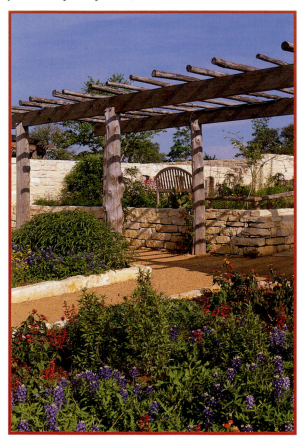

The child of the East Texas countryside had a great desire to see America's native plants put to widespread use: they are inexpensive and they belong to this country. But she realized that most people don't have reliable information about planting and cultivating the many different types of available plants. The basic need was a national center to study and share this knowledge.

She contributed 60 acres (24 hectares) of land 10 miles (16 km) east of Austin and $125,000 seed money to start the center. She asked old friends from the White House "beautification days" to help encourage the use of native plants, trees, shrubs, and wildflowers in landscaping plans for the country.

Most important, Lady Bird believed that all parts of the nation should have their own native flowers and plants, so that they would "look like themselves. When I go to Mississippi, I want to see mountain laurel and azaleas. . . . I want to keep our national heritage of wildflowers and native plants alive for generations that follow."

The Wildflower Farm in Charlotte, Vermont, helps carry out Lady Bird's desire for each state to plant and care for its own native plants.

Prickly pear cactus in Big Bend National Park

Now in a new location west of Austin, the National Wildflower Research Center has a greenhouse and many experimental plots in which to grow different plants. Staff members monitor, keep records, and do extensive research. They offer information wherever it is needed. The center encourages the breeding of wildflowers—along roadsides, in public parks, on the roughs of golf courses, and along the entrances of leisure-home developments throughout the nation.

Through her years of involvement with native blooms, Mrs. Johnson made it clear that although it is not hard to establish wildflowers, it is "chancy and not immediate." But once they are established in a particular place, they require simple maintenance, little or no herbicides or pesticides, and no fertilizer. They can get along on rainwater. They are an ecologically sound, low-cost way to make the roads and parks flower. They are not only beautiful, they also reverse harm to the environment.

Today's wildflowers are a great mixture of species from nearly everywhere on earth with our own native plants, some of which are the most beautiful in the world. According to botanist Carlton Lees, who worked with Mrs. Johnson in setting up the center, foreign plants are continually being introduced into our landscape. This process can be beneficial or destructive, depending on how certain plants react to their environments, and how these environments are managed.

During its first decade, the National Wildflower Research Center grew to involve every state, twenty countries, and 18,000 members. The center, which has a $1.7-million budget, explores everything from prairie restoration to advising states how to plant wildflowers along highways. It has created savings in water, land, and work time. The center helps gardeners locate species native to their regions and learn to grow them carefully, so they don't take over and crowd out cultivated blooms.

Lady Bird Johnson has long believed that wildflowers belong to everyone—private citizens, park managers, and people who develop land for real estate use. She and her NWRC colleagues understand the old

92

Among the wildflowers in this Hales Corners, Wisconsin, field are purple coneflowers and rattlesnake master.

A field of Texas bluebonnets

axiom that one person's orchid is another's weed—and that a weed is simply a plant that isn't in its proper setting.

Some of America's loveliest blooms were wildflowers in their native countries, while many of our home-grown plants are prized in Europe and other foreign regions. There is a difference between plants that are indigenous, or native, and those that are introduced into an area. The goal is to make sure that the plants that are introduced into our landscape are right for that area and do not destroy others around them.

Lady Bird Johnson believes firmly in the ambitious goals of the National Wildflower Research Center: to learn as much as possible about wildflower breeding and cultivation and to be a clearinghouse to spread that knowledge. She realizes it is not an easy task, noting in *Wildflowers Across America*:

"This is a pioneering effort, and sometimes I feel overwhelmed with a sense of so much to do and so little time, because of all we need to discover. Yet I can hardly wait for spring each year! Already we are on the road

Blazing star and goldenrod thrive in Markham Prairie, Illinois.

Wildflowers bloom next to the expanses of sand at Abbotts Lagoon in Point Reyes, California.

Lady Bird and Lyndon Johnson at the LBJ Ranch on their 38th wedding anniversary

This 1994 photograph of Lady Bird was taken at the U.S. Botanic Gardens in Washington, D.C.

to unlocking some of the secrets of wildflowers and to assuring their bounty in our landscapes for generations to come."

The little girl who eagerly awaited spring in East Texas grew up to become a woman who worked to spread beauty throughout her country, and then spearheaded an effort to make the most of the nation's natural plants and blooms.

Lyndon Baines Johnson once commented that he would have been content to be a "conservation president," if he hadn't had to deal with the existing problems of the cities, health care, and, of course, the Vietnam War. But he took great pride in the accomplishments of his wife, whom he strongly encouraged in her environmental efforts.

"I believe that Lady Bird touched a fundamental chord in the American people with her quiet crusade to beautify our country. She enriched the lives of all Americans," he wrote in his book *Vantage Point*. The work of the president and First Lady to place the enjoyment of nature within the reach of more of our citizens demonstrates

Preserving Nature's Medicine Cabinet

★ ★ ★ ★ ★ ★ ★ ★ ★ ★ ★ ★ ★ ★ ★ ★ ★ ★ ★ ★

The United States is home to about 25,000 native plants, from amaranth to yucca. Today, approximately 430 of these are on the brink of extinction and have been included on the Endangered Species List. More than 90 are considered threatened, 3,000 rare. Although some species of wild plants decline due to natural causes— weather, fragility, and so on—most are threatened by human activities. Overgrazing and intensive agriculture, real estate development, roadbuilding, and pollution are just some of the enemies of rare wildflowers and plants. Why all the fuss? As part of the American landscape, plants such as the salt-marsh bird's beak of California and the green pitcher plant of Alabama deserve to be preserved. But their value goes beyond their beauty. Native Americans used more than 150 native plants as medicine, and from many of these have come modern drugs and cures. The bark of the willow, for instance, contains salicylic acid, from which aspirin is made. Today, more than 120 prescription drugs are obtained from plants. Many other compounds originally found in wild plants can now be made in the laboratory. The Pacific yew gave us the drug taxol, a powerful treatment for cancer that is now artificially produced.

remarkable teamwork between a president and his First Lady.

Lady Bird had supported her husband from his earliest days in politics, and was always available to him and to their children, literally in sickness and in health. That she was able to continue in this role and at the same time carve out a significant role for herself is a testament to her energy, determination, and vision.

Decades after her tenure as First Lady, Lady Bird Johnson's contributions continue to grow and flourish.

★ ★ ★ ★ ★ ★ ★ ★ ★ ★ ★ ★ ★ ★ ★ ★ ★ ★

The Presidents and Their First Ladies

YEARS IN OFFICE			
President	*Birth–Death*	*First Lady*	*Birth–Death*
1789–1797			
George Washington	1732–1799	Martha Dandridge Custis Washington	1731–1802
1797–1801			
John Adams	1735–1826	Abigail Smith Adams	1744–1818
1801–1809			
Thomas Jefferson†	1743–1826		
1809–1817			
James Madison	1751–1836	Dolley Payne Todd Madison	1768–1849
1817–1825			
James Monroe	1758–1831	Elizabeth Kortright Monroe	1768–1830
1825–1829			
John Quincy Adams	1767–1848	Louisa Catherine Johnson Adams	1775–1852
1829–1837			
Andrew Jackson†	1767–1845		
1837–1841			
Martin Van Buren†	1782–1862		
1841			
William Henry Harrison‡	1773–1841		
1841–1845			
John Tyler	1790–1862	Letitia Christian Tyler (1841–1842)	1790–1842
		Julia Gardiner Tyler (1844–1845)	1820–1889
1845–1849			
James K. Polk	1795–1849	Sarah Childress Polk	1803–1891
1849–1850			
Zachary Taylor	1784–1850	Margaret Mackall Smith Taylor	1788–1852
1850–1853			
Millard Fillmore	1800–1874	Abigail Powers Fillmore	1798–1853
1853–1857			
Franklin Pierce	1804–1869	Jane Means Appleton Pierce	1806–1863
1857–1861			
James Buchanan*	1791–1868		
1861–1865			
Abraham Lincoln	1809–1865	Mary Todd Lincoln	1818–1882
1865–1869			
Andrew Johnson	1808–1875	Eliza McCardle Johnson	1810–1876
1869–1877			
Ulysses S. Grant	1822–1885	Julia Dent Grant	1826–1902
1877–1881			
Rutherford B. Hayes	1822–1893	Lucy Ware Webb Hayes	1831–1889
1881			
James A. Garfield	1831–1881	Lucretia Rudolph Garfield	1832–1918
1881–1885			
Chester A. Arthur†	1829–1886		

† wife died before he took office   ‡ wife too ill to accompany him to Washington   * never married

1885–1889			
Grover Cleveland	1837–1908	Frances Folsom Cleveland	1864–1947
1889–1893			
Benjamin Harrison	1833–1901	Caroline Lavinia Scott Harrison	1832–1892
1893–1897			
Grover Cleveland	1837–1908	Frances Folsom Cleveland	1864–1947
1897–1901			
William McKinley	1843–1901	Ida Saxton McKinley	1847–1907
1901–1909			
Theodore Roosevelt	1858–1919	Edith Kermit Carow Roosevelt	1861–1948
1909–1913			
William Howard Taft	1857–1930	Helen Herron Taft	1861–1943
1913–1921			
Woodrow Wilson	1856–1924	Ellen Louise Axson Wilson (1913–1914)	1860–1914
		Edith Bolling Galt Wilson (1915–1921)	1872–1961
1921–1923			
Warren G. Harding	1865–1923	Florence Kling Harding	1860–1924
1923–1929			
Calvin Coolidge	1872–1933	Grace Anna Goodhue Coolidge	1879–1957
1929–1933			
Herbert Hoover	1874–1964	Lou Henry Hoover	1874–1944
1933–1945			
Franklin D. Roosevelt	1882–1945	Anna Eleanor Roosevelt	1884–1962
1945–1953			
Harry S. Truman	1884–1972	Bess Wallace Truman	1885–1982
1953–1961			
Dwight D. Eisenhower	1890–1969	Mamie Geneva Doud Eisenhower	1896–1979
1961–1963			
John F. Kennedy	1917–1963	Jacqueline Bouvier Kennedy	1929–1994
1963–1969			
Lyndon B. Johnson	1908–1973	Claudia Taylor (Lady Bird) Johnson	1912–
1969–1974			
Richard Nixon	1913–1994	Patricia Ryan Nixon	1912–1993
1974–1977			
Gerald Ford	1913–	Elizabeth Bloomer Ford	1918–
1977–1981			
James Carter	1924–	Rosalynn Smith Carter	1927–
1981–1989			
Ronald Reagan	1911–	Nancy Davis Reagan	1923–
1989–1993			
George Bush	1924–	Barbara Pierce Bush	1925–
1993–			
William Jefferson Clinton	1946–	Hillary Rodham Clinton	1947–

Claudia Taylor (Lady Bird) Johnson Timeline

1912	★	*Titanic* sinks in the North Atlantic
		Woodrow Wilson is elected president
		New Mexico and Arizona become states
		Claudia Taylor is born on December 22
1914	★	World War I begins
1916	★	Woodrow Wilson is reelected president
1917	★	United States enters World War I
1918	★	United States and its allies win World War I
1920	★	Warren G. Harding is elected president
		Woodrow Wilson wins the Nobel Peace Prize
1923	★	Calvin Coolidge becomes president upon the death of Warren G. Harding
1927	★	Charles Lindbergh makes the first nonstop, solo flight across the Atlantic Ocean
1928	★	Herbert Hoover is elected president
		Walt Disney releases the first Mickey Mouse animated cartoon
1929	★	Stock market crashes and the Great Depression begins
1931	★	"The Star-Spangled Banner" becomes the national anthem
		Empire State Building is opened
1932	★	Franklin D. Roosevelt is elected president
		Amelia Earhart becomes the first woman to fly solo across the Atlantic Ocean
1933	★	President Roosevelt begins the New Deal to end the Great Depression
		Claudia Taylor graduates from the University of Texas

1934	★	Nylon is invented
		Claudia Taylor marries Lyndon B. Johnson
1935	★	Congress passes the Social Security Act
1936	★	Franklin D. Roosevelt is reelected president
1937	★	Lyndon B. Johnson is elected to the U.S. House of Representatives
		Golden Gate Bridge in San Francisco is dedicated
1939	★	World War II begins
1940	★	Franklin D. Roosevelt is reelected president
1941	★	Japan bombs Pearl Harbor and the United States enters World War II
1943	★	Claudia (Lady Bird) Johnson purchases her first radio station in Texas
1944	★	Lynda Bird Johnson is born
		Franklin D. Roosevelt is reelected president
1945	★	Franklin D. Roosevelt dies
		Harry S. Truman becomes president
		Germany and Japan surrender, ending World War II
1947	★	Jackie Robinson becomes the first African-American to play major-league baseball
		Luci Baines Johnson is born

1948	★	Harry S. Truman is elected president
		Lyndon B. Johnson is elected to the U.S. Senate
1949	★	United Nations headquarters is dedicated in New York City
1950	★	United States enters Korean War
1951	★	Lady Bird and Lyndon B. Johnson buy the LBJ Ranch
1952	★	Dwight D. Eisenhower is elected president
1953	★	Korean War ends
1954	★	Supreme Court declares segregated schools to be unconstitutional

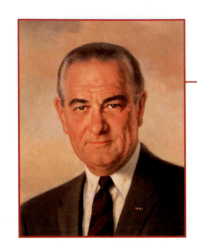

1956	★	Dwight D. Eisenhower is reelected president
1959	★	Alaska and Hawaii become states
1960	★	John F. Kennedy is elected president
		Lyndon B. Johnson is elected vice president
1961	★	Berlin Wall separates East and West Berlin
		First Americans fly in space
		United States sends aid and advisors to South Vietnam
1963	★	John F. Kennedy is assassinated
		Lyndon B. Johnson becomes president
1964	★	Congress passes and President Johnson signs the Civil Rights Act
		Lyndon B. Johnson is elected president
1965	★	Malcolm X is assassinated
		U.S. sends troops to Vietnam
		Riots break out in Los Angeles' Watts neighborhood
1966	★	Congress passes and President Johnson signs the Medicare Act
1968	★	Congress passes and President Johnson signs the Civil Rights Act
		Lyndon Johnson decides not to seek reelection
		Martin Luther King Jr. and Robert F. Kennedy are assassinated
		Richard M. Nixon is elected president
1969	★	President Nixon begins withdrawing U.S. soldiers from Vietnam
1970	★	Antiwar protests rock college campuses
1972	★	Last U.S. ground troops are withdrawn from Vietnam
		Burglary at the Watergate Complex is reported
		Richard Nixon is reelected president
1973	★	Vice President Spiro Agnew resigns
		Gerald Ford becomes vice president
1974	★	Richard M. Nixon resigns from office
		Gerald Ford becomes president

1975	★	South Vietnam falls to the Communists
1976	★	United States celebrates its bicentennial
		Jimmy Carter is elected president
1977	★	President Carter issues a pardon to Vietnam War draft evaders
1979	★	Iranians seize U.S. Embassy in Tehran and hold American hostages
1980	★	Ronald Reagan is elected president
1981	★	Iranians release the U.S. hostages
1983	★	Sally Ride becomes the first American woman astronaut in space
1984	★	Ronald Reagan is reelected president
1986	★	Space shuttle *Challenger* explodes, killing all on board
1987	★	United States and Soviet Union sign nuclear missile reduction treaty
1988	★	George Bush is elected president
1989	★	Berlin Wall comes down
1990	★	Iraq invades Kuwait
1991	★	United States leads allies in Persian Gulf War
		Iraq is pushed from Kuwait
1992	★	Bill Clinton is elected president
1993	★	Congress passes the North American Free Trade Agreement (NAFTA)
1994	★	Baseball strike cancels the World Series
1995	★	U.S. terrorists bomb the federal building in Oklahoma City, killing 168 people
		U.S. government shuts down because Congress and President Clinton cannot agree on funding
1996	★	Bill Clinton is reelected president
1998	★	Iraq agrees to weapons' inspections by UN team after United States threatens bombings

Fast Facts about
Claudia Taylor (Lady Bird) Johnson

Born: December 22, 1912, in Karnack, Texas

Parents: Thomas Taylor and Minnie Patillo Taylor

Education: One-room school in Karnack; graduated from Marshall County High School (1928); attended St. Mary's Episcopal School for Girls (a junior college in Dallas); received a bachelor of arts degree from the University of Texas in Austin (1933); received a degree in journalism and a teaching certificate from the University of Texas (1934)

Career: Bought, owned, and operated radio and television stations that she formed into the Texas Broadcasting Corporation

Marriage: To Lyndon Baines Johnson on November 17, 1934, until his death in 1973

Children: Lynda Bird Johnson and Luci Baines Johnson

Places She Lived: Karnack, Texas (1912–1934); Dallas and Austin, Texas (1928–1934); Washington, D.C. (1934–1969); LBJ Ranch near Johnson City, Texas (1951–present)

Major Achievements:

* Campaigned for her husband and helped win the southern vote for the Kennedy-Johnson ticket in 1960 and for her husband's election as president in 1964.

* As the vice president's wife, traveled to many countries and hosted foreign guests at The Elms in Washington, D.C., and at the LBJ Ranch in Texas.

* Kept a diary of her life in the White House (1963–1969), which was published as *A White House Diary* (1970).

* Worked on and was a spokesperson for Operation Head Start to help preschool children from poor families.

* Pursued her interest in beautifying rural and urban environments by (1) working with the secretary of the interior to form the Committee for a More Beautiful Capital in 1965, (2) pressing for the passage of the Highway Beautification Act of 1965, (3) founding the National Wildlife Research Center in Austin, Texas, in 1982, and (4) co-authoring *Wildflowers Across America* in 1988.